EPHESIANS

TRANSFORMED IN CHRIST

Other studies in the Not Your Average Bible Study series

Ruth

Psalms

Jonah

Malachi

Sermon on the Mount

Colossians

Hebrews

James

1 Peter

2 Peter and Jude

1–3 John

For updates on this series, visit lexhampress.com/nyab

EPHESIANS

TRANSFORMED IN CHRIST

NOT YOUR AVERAGE BIBLE STUDY

MILES CUSTIS

Ephesians: Transformed in Christ
Not Your Average Bible Study

Copyright 2014 Lexham Press

Lexham Press, 1313 Commercial St., Bellingham, WA 98225
LexhamPress.com

ISBN 978-1-57-799551-7

Editor-in-Chief: John D. Barry
Managing Editor: Rebecca Van Noord
Assistant Editors: Jessi Strong, Elizabeth Vince, and Joel Wilcox
Cover Design: Christine Gerhart
Typesetting: projectluz.com

CONTENTS

HOW TO USE THIS RESOURCE

Not Your Average Bible Study is a series of in-depth Bible studies that can be used for individual or group study. Depending on your individual needs or your group pace, you may opt to cover one lesson a week or more.

Each lesson prompts you to dig deep into the Word—as such, we recommend you use your preferred translation with this study. The author used his own translation, but included quotations from the English Standard Version. Whatever Bible version you use, please be sure you leave ample time to get into the Bible itself.

To assist you, we recommend using the Faithlife Study Bible, which contains notes written by Miles Custis and is also edited by John D. Barry. You can download this digital resource for free for your tablet, phone, personal computer, or use it online. Go to FaithlifeBible.com to learn more.

May God bless you in the study of His Word.

INTRODUCTION

In his letter to the Ephesians, Paul shows how God brought us from being "dead in trespasses and sins" (2:1-3) to being "alive together with Christ" (2:4-10). Then, he brings this truth to bear on everyday life. As believers we must "put off the old self," characterized by ignorance and selfishness, and put on the "new self," created in the likeness of God (4:17-24). Because Christ has loved us, we can now "walk in love" (5:2).

EPHESIANS 1–2

The modern church seems fragmented and divided. By some estimates, 41,000 Christian denominations and organizations exist worldwide.[1] The numbers seem to clash with Paul's description of the church as Christ's body (Eph 1:22–23) and God's temple (2:19–22). He stresses that believers should be united in Christ—can the modern Church, with its thousands of separate denominations, really display the type of unity Paul writes about in Ephesians?

Paul believed unity is achieved through our attitudes and actions toward each other (4:1–6). By becoming more Christ-like, we can grow in our unity (4:15–16). This requires that each of us put off our old self and put on the new self, which is characterized by love, truthfulness, kindness, forgiveness and submission to one another (4:22–32; 5:21). Only when each believer models Christ's love can the Church experience the unity Paul describes. In the next eight studies, we will explore how Paul explains God's work of salvation and how that work should foster unity among believers.

---

1 Based on research by the Pew Forum and the Center for the Study of Global Christianity in 2011. For a full report on global Christianity, visit PewForum.org.

READING EPHESIANS

Pray that God will give you wisdom as you study the Letter of Ephesians.

Read the entire Letter of Ephesians aloud in one sitting.

Reading the Bible aloud allows you to interact with the text differently. Ephesians was likely read aloud as it was circulated among a number of house churches in Ephesus and other cities in Asia Minor.

As you read Ephesians, write down recurring themes. When Paul describes unity, how does he refer to the unity of believers?

_____

_____

_____

Underline each occurrence of the word "love" in the letter. Paul refers to both God's love for us and our love for others. When does he refer to each one, and how are these aspects of love related to unity?

_____

_____

_____

Underline each time Paul says "in Christ." Think about your own faith community and your role within it. How can you help ensure that your church is unified?

_____

_____

_____

Paul often mentions the three members of the Trinity. How does he describe the roles of God the Father, Jesus Christ and the Holy Spirit? How do these roles relate to unity?

_____

_____

_____

What things are "in Christ"?

_____

_____

_____

ADOPTED AND REDEEMED

Pray that God would make you holy and blameless before Him.

Read Ephesians 1:1–14. Reflect on verses 1:1–10.

After an opening greeting, Paul presents a lengthy blessing—Ephesians 1:3–14 is one sentence in Greek—where he praises God for what He has done. How does Paul describe God's work?

_____

_____

_____

_____

What does it mean to be blessed in Christ "with every spiritual blessing" (see 2 Pet 1:3–4)?

_____

_____

_____

_____

In Ephesians 1:4–5, Paul speaks of God as choosing and predestining us. Does God's choosing of us say anything about us (also read 1 Cor 1:27–29)? Why did God choose us?

_____

_____

_____

_____

Compare this passage with 1 Peter 1:14–16. What does it mean to be "holy and blameless"? Does this phrase describe you? Read Ephesians 5:25–27. In what ways are you holy and blameless?

_____

_____

_____

_____

According to 1:5, why did God predestine us? Adoption in the ancient world allowed the adoptee to share in the inheritance (compare Rom 8:15–17). Read Galatians 4:4–7. How was our adoption made possible?

_____

_____

_____

_____

What is the purpose of adoption, and what are the benefits of being adopted as children of God (Eph 1:6)? Take time to praise God for His grace in adopting you as His child.

_____

_____

_____

Paul describes the work of Christ in 1:7–10. What does it mean to have "redemption through His blood"?

_____

_____

_____

_____

Redemption meant paying a ransom to free slaves (Lev 25:47–50). How does this relate to our redemption (compare Mark 10:45; 1 Cor 6:20; Gal 5:13)?

_____

_____

_____

What is the relationship between redemption and forgiveness? (see Col 1:13–14).

_____

_____

_____

OUR INHERITANCE

Pray that the Holy Spirit would help you live in praise of God's glory.

Read Ephesians 1:1–14. Reflect on verses 1:11–14.

Ephesians 1:11–14 continues the single Greek sentence that began in 1:3. Paul mentions the inheritance we have received in Christ. How does our inheritance relate to our adoption?

_____

_____

_____

_____

Read Romans 8:12–17. What does it mean to live as children of God? What are the implications of being a fellow heir with Christ?

_____

_____

_____

_____

In Ephesians 1:13–14, Paul describes the role the Holy Spirit plays in our inheritance. In what way is the Spirit "the guarantee" of our inheritance (see 2 Cor 1:21–22)?

_____

_____

_____

_____

A seal was a sign of ownership or a means of identification. How does the work of the Holy Spirit in your life identify you as a child of God?

_____

_____

_____

Read about the fruit of the Spirit in Galatians 5:22–23. How can you better display these characteristics in your life (compare Gal 6:8–10)?

_____

_____

_____

In Ephesians 1:11, Paul says that God "works all things according to the counsel of His will." How do you understand this passage when you are suffering (see Gen 50:20; Jas 1:2–4)?

_____

_____

_____

How does being a co-heir with Christ influence how you respond to suffering or trials (see Rom 8:17; 2 Tim 2:11–13)?

_____

_____

_____

The phrase "to the praise of His glory" is repeated in Ephesians 1:12 and 1:14 (see also 1:6). In what ways does God's work of salvation in you cause "the praise of His glory"? What steps can you take to ensure you are living in a way that praises God?

_____

_____

_____

THE HOPE OF GOD'S CALLING

Pray that God would grant you wisdom and knowledge.

Read Ephesians 1:1–23. Reflect on verses 1:15–23.

After praising God for His work of salvation (1:3–14), Paul turns his attention to the Ephesian believers. He mentions his thanksgiving and prayers for them—prayers that God would give them wisdom and knowledge. What is the focus of the wisdom and knowledge that Paul prays the Ephesians will gain? How do you seek more knowledge of God?

_____

_____

_____

_____

In the New Testament, hope conveys an expectation that God will provide. What is the hope of God's calling (1:18)? How can you know it more (see 1 Pet 3:15)?

_____

_____

_____

Read how Paul describes hope in Romans 5:2–5. How is hope related to suffering (Romans 5:4; compare Matt 5:12)? How can your hope in God's calling help you rejoice in your suffering?

_____

_____

_____

Paul refers to "the surpassing greatness of his power toward us who believe" in Ephesians 1:19. How is God's mighty strength shown in Christ's resurrection (compare Rom 1:4; 1 Cor 15:12–22; 2 Cor 13:4; Col 2:12–13)?

_____

_____

_____

In Ephesians 1:22–23, Paul describes the church as Christ's body. When you reflect on this, how does it encourage you to seek unity within your local church?

_____

_____

_____

Read 1 Corinthians 12:12–27. Note how Paul describes the individual roles people play within the body of Christ. Does this describe your church? How are you contributing to this unity?

_____

_____

_____

How does unity glorify Christ, the head of the church (see also Eph 4:15–16)? In what ways can you encourage this type of unity in your church?

_____

_____

_____

DEAD IN TRESPASSES AND SINS

✋ *Pray that God would keep you from following selfish desires.*

📄 *Read Ephesians 1:15–2:10. Reflect on verses 2:1–3.*

In this section, Paul describes the Ephesian believers' condition before the work of Christ as being dead in their trespasses and sins. How would you define the phrase "dead in trespasses and sins"?

_____

_____

_____

_____

Those who are physically dead do not have power to give themselves life. What are the implications for those who are spiritually dead (compare Col 2:13–14)?

_____

_____

_____

Paul goes on to describe the lifestyle of the unbeliever. What does it mean to follow "the course of this world" (Eph 2:2)?

_____

_____

_____

How would you describe "the world" (see Col 2:8; Jas 1:27, 4:4; 1 John 2:15–16), and what is its appeal? How can you keep yourself from following the world?

_____

_____

_____

_____

Who is "the ruler of the authority of the air" (Eph 2:2)? What is this ruler's connection to the world (see John 12:31)? How can you resist this ruler (see Eph 6:11–18)?

_____

_____

_____

_____

In 2:3, Paul describes our former nature. What does it mean to follow the desires of the body and the mind?

_____

_____

_____

_____

Paul often talks about the works of the flesh. Read Galatians 5:19–21, 1 Corinthians 3:1–3, and Colossians 3:5–11. What stands out to you from these lists? How does the flesh work against unity?

_____

_____

_____

_____

Ephesians 2:1–3 describes how believers were before they received Christ. Do any aspects of this description still apply to you? What steps can you take to ensure that you are no longer living this way? Who can encourage you and hold you accountable?

_____

_____

_____

Read Ephesians 4:20–32. What does Paul instruct the Ephesians to do to put off the old self?

_____

_____

_____

ALIVE IN CHRIST

✋ *Pray that your works would reflect Christ's love to others.*

📄 *Read Ephesians 2:1–10. Reflect on verses 2:4–10.*

Beginning in 2:4, Paul contrasts the believers' new state (2:4–10) with their previous condition of being "dead in trespasses and sin" (2:1–3). The change in condition is entirely God's doing: "But God … made us alive together with Christ." What reason does Paul give for God's actions?

_____

_____

_____

Reflect on the nature of God's love as you read John 3:16, Romans 5:5–8, 8:35–39, and 1 John 4:9–10. What do these passages tell you about God's love?

_____

_____

_____

Later, Paul instructs the Ephesians to imitate God—specifically, God's love (Eph 5:1–2). Read John 13:34–35, 1 Corinthians 13:4–13, Colossians 3:14, and 1 John 4:11–12. What do these passages say about how we should love others? How does this type of love foster unity among believers?

_____

_____

_____

_____

Write down three ways you can show God's love to others.

1. _____

2. _____

3. _____

Twice in this section of Ephesians, Paul says "by grace you are saved" (Eph 2:5, 8). Why is this important? Who would get the praise or glory if salvation was earned through works (see also Rom 4:2, 16)?

_____

_____

_____

_____

What role do works play in the life of a believer (see Eph 2:10; Titus 3:5, 8)?

_____

_____

_____

_____

Paul describes believers as God's "workmanship" or "creation" (Eph 2:10). This term occurs only one other place in the New Testament. In Romans 1:20, Paul refers to the "things created" that show God's invisible attributes. As described in Ephesians 2:10, what is the purpose of the believer's creation in Christ? How do your good works show God's attributes?

_____

_____

_____

_____

RECONCILED TO GOD

Praise God for the reconciliation provided by Christ's sacrifice.

Read Ephesians 2:1–18. Reflect on verses 2:11–18.

The word "therefore" at the beginning of 2:11 points back to the previous section (Eph 2:1–10). What does Paul want the Ephesians to remember?

_____

_____

_____

In the Old Testament, the Israelites were often instructed to remember what God had done for them (see Exod 13:3; Deut 5:15; 15:15). How does remembering what God has done for you encourage you in difficult times?

_____

_____

_____

_____

Paul makes the point that Christ's sacrifice has brought Gentiles (non-Jewish people) into the same position as Jews (Eph 2:14); it has also abolished the law (2:15) and allowed Gentiles to enjoy "the covenants of promise" (2:12). What are "the covenants of promise"?

_____

_____

_____

_____

Read Genesis 17:4–6, Romans 4:13–17, 15:8–13, 2 Corinthians 1:19–20, and Galatians 3:16–18. How did Christ confirm God's promise? What does God's promise rest on?

_____

_____

_____

From what did God save us, and how (see Eph 2:1–3)? What does it mean to reconcile something (see Rom 5:10–11; 2 Cor 5:18–20; Col 1:21–23)?

_____

_____

_____

What roles do the different members of the Trinity play in Ephesians 1:13–18?

_____

_____

_____

Paul emphasizes unity in this passage. What is the "peace" that Christ preached (2:17)? How should this peace encourage unity (see Eph 4:3; Col 3:15)?

_____

_____

_____

If you have difficult relationships with any believers, what steps can you take to be reconciled to them?

_____

_____

_____

GOD'S DWELLING PLACE

Pray that the Spirit would help you reflect God as His temple.

Read Ephesians 2:1–22. Reflect on verses 2:19–22.

Throughout Ephesians 2, Paul contrasts in various ways the state of believers before Christ with their changed status in Christ (2:1–3, 4–10, 11–12, 13–18). In 2:19, he describes how the status of a non-Jewish believer is changed through Christ's work of reconciliation. How do "strangers and foreigners" compare with "fellow citizens"?

_____

_____

_____

In New Testament times, having Roman citizenship meant extra rights and protections (see Acts 16:38–39; 22:27–29). What are the rights and protections of heavenly citizenship (see Phil 3:20–21)?

_____

_____

_____

Paul uses the image of a building to describe the household of God. In what way are "the apostles and prophets" the foundation of the Church (see Eph 3:4–6; 4:11–13; 1 Cor 12:27–31)? How is Jesus Christ the cornerstone (Acts 4:11–12; 1 Pet 2:4–8)? What is your role in the church (1 Pet 2:5)?

_____

_____

_____

Paul describes "the building" as "a holy temple" and "a dwelling place for God." In ancient Israel, the temple represented the presence of God on earth (see 1 Kgs 9:3; Psa 18:6; Hab 2:20). The Israelites directed their prayers toward the temple (Psa 138:2; Dan 6:10) and considered it a place of great holiness (1 Kgs 8:10–11). Reflect on the importance of the physical temple. What are the implications of believers now being God's temple (see 2 Cor 6:16–7:1)? How do believers represent the presence of God on earth?

_____

_____

_____

Knowing believers are a representation of God, do you think you are living as a holy temple? What can you do to become a better dwelling place for God?

_____

_____

_____

CONCLUSION

In the first two chapters of Ephesians, Paul emphasizes God's work of salvation in believers. He explains how God took us from spiritual death to life in Christ (2:1–10). As he discusses this, Paul shows how God's work of salvation perfectly illustrates unity. Each member of the Trinity has an active role: God the Father chose us (1:3–6), Christ redeemed us by His blood (1:7–12) and the Holy Spirit is the seal of our inheritance (1:13–14). It is through the work of the Trinity that we as believers can enjoy reconciliation with God. Through this reconciliation, we all become part of the same unified body—God's temple. May you recognize God's work in your life and live in a way that brings honor and glory to Him. In doing so, may you bring unity among Christ's followers.

EPHESIANS 3-4

The Bible tells who God is and what He has done. But it's easy to forget what we've learned after we close our Bibles, swallow our last drop of coffee and start our day. God's Word should transform us. His work of salvation should affect our thoughts, our actions and our relationships with others.

In Ephesians, Paul seeks to show God's transformative work. In the first three chapters, he lays out God's plan for salvation—how God brought us from being "dead in trespasses and sins" (2:1-3) to being "alive together with Christ" (2:4-10). He explains how God chose to include the Gentiles (non-Jewish people) in His plan of salvation so that all might become fellow heirs of His promises (2:11-22).

In the second half of Ephesians, Paul brings the fullness of this truth to bear on everyday life. He says that as believers we must "put off the old self," characterized by ignorance and selfishness, and put on the "new self," created in the likeness of God (4:17-24). This changes our entire orientation. Instead of fulfilling our own needs, we are prompted to put others' needs first. In doing so, we maintain the unity of the Spirit and help build up the body of Christ.

In Part I, we looked at Paul's teaching on the unity of believers. We examined God's work of salvation and saw how it illustrates unity. We learned that God wants us to be unified as believers as we are reconciled to Him. In these next eight studies, we will see how Paul understood the surpassing love of Christ and how we should live in light of that love.

REREADING EPHESIANS

Pray that God will open His Word to you as you study the Letter of Ephesians.

Read the entire Letter of Ephesians aloud in one sitting.

The letter to the Ephesians likely would have been read aloud since it circulated among the churches in Asia Minor. Reading aloud enables you to experience the letter as the original recipients did. As you read, underline instructions Paul gives his audience. How do these instructions help you live for Christ? Once again, note Paul's emphasis on unity in Ephesians.

_____

_____

_____

_____

Throughout the letter, Paul contrasts the believers' condition before Christ with their condition after Christ. What characterizes those who are "in Christ"? How should they live?

_____

_____

_____

_____

_____

According to Paul, what can help believers live as new creations in Christ? Who does he offer as an example to imitate?

_____

_____

_____

Think of someone in your life who exemplifies living in Christ, and list some of their characteristics. How can you cultivate the same attitudes or behaviors in your own life?

_____

_____

_____

THE MYSTERY OF CHRIST

Pray that the Spirit will guide you in fulfilling God's plan for your life.

Read Ephesians 2:1–3:7. Reflect on verses 3:1–7.

In Ephesians 2, Paul emphasized that Gentiles (non-Jewish people) have become fellow citizens and have been brought into God's covenant promises. In the next section, he discusses his role in God's plan, claiming that he has been given the stewardship of God's grace (3:2). The Greek word for "stewardship" (oikonomia, οἰκονομία) is the same word used for "plan" or "administration" in 1:10 and 3:9. As a steward of God's grace, Paul seeks to carry out God's plans. Are you actively seeking to carry out God's plan in your life? What steps can you take to become a more effective steward of God's grace?

_____

_____

_____

_____

_____

_____

In 3:4, Paul writes that he intends to give "insight into the mystery of Christ." According to 3:6, what is this mystery?

_____

_____

_____

_____

_____

Paul uses three different terms to describe how Gentiles are included in the gospel: "fellow heirs," "fellow members of the body," and "fellow sharers of the promise." Read 1 Corinthians 12:12–26. Make a list of what it means to be members of one body. How do these things influence the way you view your role in God's plan? How should they influence your attitude toward other believers?

_____

_____

_____

In describing believers as "fellow heirs" and "sharers of the promise in Christ Jesus," Paul likely is referring to God's promise to Abraham (see Gen 12:1–3; 17:1–8). Read Galatians 3:14–4:7. What does this passage say about being an heir to the promise? What are the benefits of being a child rather than a slave?

_____

_____

_____

HUMILITY AND BOLDNESS

Pray that God would give you boldness to proclaim His Word.

Read Ephesians 2:11–3:13. Reflect on verses 3:8–13.

After describing his role as a steward of God's grace, Paul emphasizes how unworthy he is of that calling, claiming to be "the least of all the saints" (3:8). Elsewhere he calls himself "the least of the apostles, not worthy to be called an apostle" (1 Cor 15:9) and the worst of sinners (1 Tim 1:15). Why would Paul emphasize his unworthiness?

_____

_____

_____

What does God's work through someone like Paul communicate about Christ's redeeming power (compare 1 Cor 15:10)?

_____

_____

_____

Have you ever felt like God couldn't use you to accomplish His purposes? Some of the most unlikely characters in the Bible were used in God's plan (e.g., Exod 4; Josh 2; Ruth 1–4). Identify other verses or stories that affirm that God can use anyone.

_____

_____

_____

_____

If Paul considered himself the least of the saints and the foremost sinner, where did he get boldness to preach the gospel (see Eph 3:11–12; compare 2 Cor 3:4–6)?

_____

_____

_____

In light of his humility, what does Paul's courage teach you? Make a list of ways you can be more bold in sharing your faith.

_____

_____

_____

Later in Ephesians, Paul asks for prayer that he would have boldness to proclaim the mystery of the gospel (see 6:19). Do you pray for courage to proclaim God's Word? Spend time in prayer asking God for both the heart and the confidence to speak about Him and His saving work.

_____

_____

_____

A PRAYER FOR THE LOVE OF CHRIST

✋ *Pray that Christ's love would dwell in your heart.*

📄 *Read Ephesians 3:1–21. Reflect on verses 3:14–21.*

In this section, Paul picks up the thought that he began in 3:1. He prays that the Ephesian believers would be strengthened in their inner person, that Christ will dwell in their hearts, and that they will be strong enough to grasp Christ's immense love. Note that in this section, Paul mentions all three members of the Godhead: God the Father, Jesus Christ and the Holy Spirit. What roles or attributes does he ascribe to each?

_____

_____

_____

_____

_____

In his prayer that Christ would dwell in the hearts of the Ephesian believers (3:17), Paul uses the Greek word *katoikeō* (κατοικέω), which refers to settling down or permanently residing somewhere. What does it mean to have Christ residing in you?

_____

_____

_____

_____

_____

In what ways should His presence affect the way you live (see 4:17–24)? What can you do to remember that Christ is dwelling in you?

_____

_____

_____

_____

Paul wants the Ephesian believers to understand just how wide, long, high and deep Christ's love is (3:18). Yet if the love of Christ "surpasses knowledge" (3:19), how can we know it?

_____

_____

_____

_____

The Greek word for "knowledge" (gnosis, γνῶσις) often refers to knowledge gained through experience. In what ways have you experienced the love of Christ? How do these experiences help you understand Christ's love?

_____

_____

_____

_____

Paul concludes his prayer with a benediction that gives glory to God (3:20–21). How does he describe God in these verses?

_____

_____

_____

_____

In what ways do Paul's words reassure you that God is able not only to do more than you ask, but also to do more than you can comprehend? Allow this assurance to influence your prayer life.

_____

_____

_____

INSTRUCTIONS DESIGNED FOR UNITY

Pray that God would help you live in a manner worthy of your calling.

Read Ephesians 3:1–4:16. Reflect on verses 4:1–6.

The second half of Ephesians begins with instructions, as Paul exhorts the Ephesian believers to "live in a manner worthy" of their calling (4:1). He begins with the transition with "therefore," which means he is drawing on the ideas of the previous verses. Paul could be referring back to his prayer and the surpassing love of Christ (3:14–21), the inclusion of Gentiles among the people of God (2:11–22), or the changed state believers enjoy in Christ (2:1–10). Which of these do you think Paul had in mind?

_____

_____

_____

_____

_____

_____

What does it mean to "live in a manner worthy of the calling" (4:1)? How can each declaration encourage you to carry out this instruction?

_____

_____

_____

_____

_____

Paul goes on to list behaviors that believers should embrace (4:2). Make a list of these actions and attitudes. How do they compare to the behaviors valued by Western culture?

_____

_____

_____

_____

Which of the above characteristics do you particularly struggle with?

_____

_____

_____

_____

The behaviors Paul lists in 4:2 are designed to promote unity. Name specific ways these behaviors create unity.

_____

_____

_____

_____

Note how often Paul repeats the word "one" to emphasize that we all share the same faith. How does this encourage you to display the characteristics from 4:2? How can you show more humility, gentleness, patience and love in your interactions with others?

_____

_____

_____

_____

GIFTS DESIGNED FOR EDIFYING

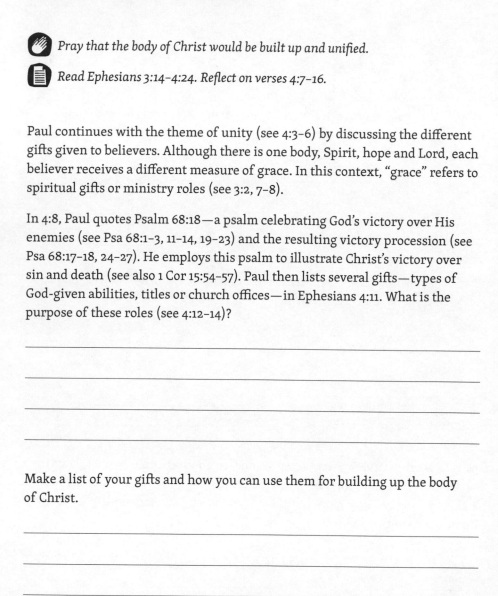

Pray that the body of Christ would be built up and unified.

Read Ephesians 3:14–4:24. Reflect on verses 4:7–16.

Paul continues with the theme of unity (see 4:3–6) by discussing the different gifts given to believers. Although there is one body, Spirit, hope and Lord, each believer receives a different measure of grace. In this context, "grace" refers to spiritual gifts or ministry roles (see 3:2, 7–8).

In 4:8, Paul quotes Psalm 68:18—a psalm celebrating God's victory over His enemies (see Psa 68:1–3, 11–14, 19–23) and the resulting victory procession (see Psa 68:17–18, 24–27). He employs this psalm to illustrate Christ's victory over sin and death (see also 1 Cor 15:54–57). Paul then lists several gifts—types of God-given abilities, titles or church offices—in Ephesians 4:11. What is the purpose of these roles (see 4:12–14)?

_____

_____

_____

_____

Make a list of your gifts and how you can use them for building up the body of Christ.

_____

_____

_____

_____

Read Romans 12:3–8 and 1 Corinthians 12:4–14, and compare these passages with Ephesians 4:7–16. How are these passages similar? How are they different? What does Paul focus on in Romans and Corinthians?

_____

_____

_____

_____

Paul stresses that these offices and/or gifts are intended to help believers grow in maturity—a theme he emphasizes in Ephesians 4:13–14. How does he characterize immaturity?

_____

_____

_____

Earlier Paul emphasized knowledge of the love of Christ (see 3:18–19). Here he stresses that knowledge of Christ Himself is a means of gaining maturity. How does knowing Christ bring maturity? What are some ways you have matured as you have grown in your relationship with Christ?

_____

_____

_____

In concluding this section, Paul again draws on the description of believers as a body, with Christ as the head (4:15–16; compare 1:22–23). How does the body grow? How can you, as a "single part," make sure you are working for the growth of the whole body?

_____

_____

_____

PUTTING ON THE NEW SELF

Pray that you would be renewed.

Read Ephesians 4:1–32. Reflect on verses 4:17–24.

After describing the different gifts God has given to edify and unify the church, Paul returns to instruction. In 4:1, he instructed the Ephesian believers to live in a manner worthy of their calling; here he instructs them to no longer live like the Gentiles. How does Paul describe the Gentiles' lifestyle?

_____

_____

_____

_____

According to Paul, why do the Gentiles of his time have a darkened understanding and alienation from God? What is the result of this alienation (4:19)?

_____

_____

_____

_____

In Paul's view, which has more influence: someone's actions, or their thoughts? What influences your thinking?

_____

_____

_____

What does it mean to have a hardened heart (see also Exod 7:13; Psa 95:8–9)?

_____

_____

_____

How does Paul's description of the Gentiles here compare with his description of the former state of believers in Ephesians 2:1–3?

_____

_____

_____

_____

Paul contrasts living like the Gentiles with the way Ephesian believers have learned to live in Christ (4:20). He tells them to "put off the old self," be renewed and "put on the new self." How does Paul contrast the old self (4:22) and the new self (4:24)? What is the purpose of the new self?

_____

_____

_____

_____

The Greek word for "renewed" (*ananeousthai*, ἀνανεοῦσθαι; 4:23) is in the present tense, which indicates a continued action. Think of ways in which your life is being renewed. How has your thought process changed? How has your behavior changed?

_____

_____

_____

_____

CHARACTERISTICS OF THE NEW SELF

Pray that God would help you live the instructions listed in Ephesians.

Read Ephesians 4:17–5:21. Reflect on verses 4:25–32.

The transitional "therefore" in 4:25 points back to the previous section, in which Paul instructed the Ephesian believers to put off the old self and put on the new self (4:17–24). Now he offers specific ways to do these things. What is the focus of these instructions? Which of them stand out to you, and why? Pray about these instructions for your life, and ask a friend to pray for you.

_____

_____

_____

_____

Look at the reasons Paul offers for some of his instructions. According to Paul, why should we speak truth and not lie (4:25)? Why should we work with our own hands (4:28)? Instead of corrupting or foul speech, what should proceed from our mouths (4:29)?

_____

_____

_____

_____

_____

All of these instructions in 4:25–32 relate to how we treat others. They can be summed up by the second greatest commandment: "You shall love your neighbor as yourself" (see Matt 22:39; Mark 12:31; compare Rom 13:9). How do Paul's instructions encourage you to treat others as yourself? How do they influence unity among believers?

_____

_____

_____

_____

_____

Paul closes this section by reminding the Ephesian believers how God forgave them through Christ. Read Matthew 18:21–35. What does Jesus say about forgiveness?

_____

_____

_____

_____

Are there people in your life that you need to forgive? Is there someone from whom you need to ask forgiveness?

_____

_____

_____

_____

CONCLUSION

In Ephesians, Paul calls believers to put on the new self—one "created in Christ Jesus for good works" (2:10). As he clarifies what that looks like in our day-to-day lives, we find more than just instructions for individual growth; we find directions for living as members of the body of Christ. The two are tightly interwoven. How we treat one another can build up or tear down the body of Christ.

Putting on the new self pushes us to look beyond ourselves. It prompts us to consider how our attitudes and actions build up the people around us. Are your actions encouraging unity among believers or causing division? When we shift our orientation away from ourselves, we will be able to live with humility, gentleness, patience, compassion and forgiveness (4:2, 32). May you speak the truth in love as you grow in Christ. May we all reach "the unity of the faith and the knowledge of the Son of God" (4:13).

EPHESIANS 5–6

The final two chapters of Ephesians include practical, detailed instructions for several different groups: wives, husbands, children, parents, servants and masters. We often study these instructions to learn how to best fill these roles. But what if you don't fall into any of these categories? How can you apply Paul's instructions to your life?

In the Part I and II, we saw how Paul explained God's work of salvation in his letter to the Ephesians. Paul also explained how we should live as new creatures, unified through the Spirit as members of the body of Christ.

Paul's instructions in Ephesians 5:22–6:9 describe how to live a godly life within specific roles, but he begins the chapter with a command to "become imitators of God" (5:1). Paul encourages all believers to love sacrificially as Christ did, learn what pleases the Lord, and live wisely (5:2–16). Every of us is responsible to be filled with the Spirit and offer praise with thankful hearts, putting others ahead of ourselves (5:18–21).

Ultimately, all believers should strive to "become imitators of God"—our heavenly master (6:9). Only then can we be unified as the body of Christ (4:13–16). In these last eight studies, we will consider Paul's teaching to learn how we can live a Christ-centered life.

EPHESIANS: A SENSE OF THE WHOLE

Pray that God's word will influence your life.

Read the entire Letter of Ephesians aloud in one sitting.

As you read, think about the relationship between Paul's theology and his encouragement for daily living.

Notice how Paul shifts his focus in later chapters. In Ephesians 1–3 he laid out God's plan of salvation. How does that truth influence the practical advice of Ephesians 4–6? How does your view of God and His salvation influence the way you live?

BECOMING IMITATORS OF GOD

Pray that you will grow to be more like Christ in your love for fellow believers.

Read Ephesians 4:17–5:21. Reflect on verses 5:1–14.

Paul begins this section by pointing back again ("Therefore ...") to his instructions on how members of the Church should treat each other in the spirit of Christ (4:25–32). What specific behaviors should we imitate (4:32)?

_____

_____

_____

_____

Returning to 5:1–14, how does Paul call us to imitate God? What steps can we take to closely follow God's example?

_____

_____

_____

_____

In 5:2, Paul exhorts the Ephesian believers to "walk" or "live" in love. What does it mean to walk in love?

_____

_____

_____

_____

In John 13:34–35 and 15:12–17, Jesus tells the disciples to love each other as He has loved them—with a selfless love. This love should extend to the point where we are willing to make profound sacrifices (see John 15:13). What are the stakes (John 13:35)?

_____

_____

_____

_____

In Ephesians 5:3–12 Paul encourages believers to put off actions that reflect their lives before Christ, the "old way," and to take on new Christ-like behaviors. We are to "try to discern what is pleasing to the Lord" (see 5:10). What should we do when confronted with "deeds of darkness" (see 5:11)?

_____

_____

_____

_____

In writing to the Galatian church, Paul exhorts believers to live and walk "in the Spirit" so that they will not provoke each other with conceit or envy (see Gal 5:25–26). Many of the actions Paul says to avoid disrupt the unity of believers; he also encourages unity. Examine your life for selfish behavior you need to confess. What positive behaviors can you start to practice?

_____

_____

_____

_____

WALKING WISELY

Pray that you would be filled with the Spirit.

Read Ephesians 5:1–21. Reflect on verses 5:15–21.

Paul continues to encourage the Ephesian believers to imitate God in their lives (see 5:1). He instructs them to live wisely because "the days are evil" (5:15–16). Paul may mean that the days are immoral (see Eph 4:17–19; 5:3–12), hostile toward believers (see 2 Thess 1:4; 2 Tim 3:12–13), or ruled by evil powers (see Eph 2:2–3; 6:11–12). How do you view the days in which we live?

_____

_____

_____

_____

How can you be more intentional about living wisely?

_____

_____

_____

Why do you think Paul contrasts drunkenness with being filled with the Spirit (5:18)? Compare people's reactions to the coming of the Holy Spirit at Pentecost in Acts 2:13.

_____

_____

_____

_____

Paul writes that being filled with the Spirit should result in an attitude of worship and thankfulness (see Ephesians 5:19–20). Are you able to be thankful in all things?

_____

_____

_____

How could rejoicing "in the Lord always" help you in difficult situations (Phil 4:4–7)?

_____

_____

_____

Paul calls believers to "make the most of the time" (Eph 5:16), just as he does in Colossians 4:5–6. How could you make better use of your time? What connection does Paul make between wise use of our time and giving thanks (see Col 3:17)?

_____

_____

_____

OF WIVES AND HUSBANDS

Pray that God would bless believers' marriages so that they would be a testimony of Christ's love.

Read Ephesians 5:1–6:9. Reflect on verses 5:22–33.

In Ephesians 5:22–6:9, Paul gives a series of instructions to specific family members. This form of instruction—known as "household codes"—was common in the Graeco-Roman world. In Ephesians 5:22–33, Paul addresses husbands and wives, comparing their relationship to that of Christ and His Church. What parallels does Paul draw between the two? How would Christ-like characteristics make a relationship stronger?

_____

_____

_____

Paul offers instructions to wives in 5:22–24 and 5:33b. Why does he offer these instructions?

_____

_____

_____

Compare what Paul says here to his instructions in 1 Corinthians 11:3. Read Matthew 20:25–28. What does it mean to be "the head" and to have authority or "be great"?

_____

_____

_____

Read Paul's instructions to husbands in Ephesians 5:25–33. What advice does he give them?

_____

_____

_____

Paul calls marriage a "great mystery" that "refers to Christ and the church" (5:31–32). How does marriage portray that relationship? How can Christian marriages testify to unbelievers about Christ's love?

_____

_____

_____

Paul has already applied his instructions to husbands ("love your wives") and wives ("submit to your husbands") to all believers. In 5:2 he instructs believers to walk in sacrificial love, and in 5:21 he tells them to submit to one another. How can you exhibit these behaviors in your relationships with other believers?

_____

_____

_____

OF CHILDREN AND PARENTS

Pray that God would bless your relationships with your children or parents.

Read Ephesians 5:15–6:9. Reflect on verses 6:1–4.

Paul continues his household code (5:22–6:9) with instructions for children and parents. He tells children to obey their parents, and adds the phrase "in the Lord." What does he mean by this (compare 5:22 and 6:1)?

_____

_____

_____

Paul tells children to do what is "right." The word for "right" (*dikaios*, δίκαιος) is often translated "just" or "righteous" (see Matt 1:19; Rom 2:13). How is obeying one's parents "righteous"?

_____

_____

_____

_____

Paul's instructions to parents include a prohibition—"do not make your children angry"—and an alternate choice (Eph 6:4). What are the differences between the "discipline of the Lord" and a discipline that provokes anger?

_____

_____

_____

_____

A parallel passage, Colossians 3:21, warns parents not to discourage their children. Why would the Lord's discipline not be discouraging (see Prov 3:11–12; Rev 3:19)?

_____

_____

_____

Paul's household code often parallels the book of Proverbs. Read Proverbs 1:8–9, 4:1–4, and 6:20–23. What benefits do these verses describe for those who obey their fathers' instructions?

_____

_____

_____

Read Proverbs 12:1, 13:24, 19:18, 22:15, and 23:13–14. What do these verses say about discipline?

_____

_____

_____

OF SERVANTS AND MASTERS

Pray that the Holy Spirit would help you view people without partiality.

Read Ephesians 5:22–6:9. Reflect on verses 6:5–9.

The final instructions in Paul's household code are for servants and masters (6:5–9). Just as children are to obey their parents (6:1), Paul instructs servants to obey their masters (6:5). How are his instructions on obedience different for the two groups?

_____

_____

_____

Why do you think Paul emphasizes sincerity when exhorting servants to obey (6:5)? Compare this passage to Colossians 3:22. Who should be the focus of all obedience?

_____

_____

_____

_____

Referring to his instructions to servants, Paul exhorts masters to "do the same to them" (Eph 6:9). This sense of mutual respect would have been dramatically countercultural in Paul's day. What reasons does Paul give for this exhortation?

_____

_____

_____

Some people apply Paul's instructions to today's employees and employers. Do you think this is or isn't a fair comparison?

_____

_____

_____

Paul explains that God is the Lord of both the master and servant. Proverbs also points to God's creation of all people to reinforce that there should be no distinction between rich and poor (see Prov 22:2; 29:13). Compare Galatians 3:27–29. How would this concept of impartiality affect the relationship between servant and master? Does it affect how you view others (compare Jas 2:1–13)?

_____

_____

_____

BEING STRONG IN THE LORD

Pray that God would help you stand against the spiritual forces of evil.

Read Ephesians 5:22–6:20. Reflect on verses 6:10–17.

After delivering his household code (5:22–6:9), Paul addresses all believers using the analogy of the armor of God (6:10–17). Note that the qualities Paul encourages in previous verses in Ephesians—love, submission, humility and gentleness—are typically not qualities associated with warfare. What is the connection between these characteristics and being strong (6:10)? Whose strength does Paul refer to here?

_____

_____

_____

Paul may have been drawing from the Divine Warrior motif of the Old Testament. As we see in Isaiah 59:14–21, the LORD puts on armor. Why does Paul instruct the Ephesian believers to put on the armor of God?

_____

_____

_____

Read Ephesians 6:11–13 and think about how you prepare yourself (or don't) to confront the spiritual realm in spiritual warfare.

_____

_____

_____

The Greek imperatives Paul uses in this section are all plural, indicating that all believers—the Church as a collective—are to put on the armor of God. What are the connections between the specific pieces of armor and their attributes (e.g., a shield and faith)?

_____

_____

_____

PRAYING AT ALL TIMES

Pray that God would give you words to boldly proclaim the gospel.

Read Ephesians 6:10–24. Reflect on verses 6:18–24.

Whether we view prayer as the final piece of armor or as a separate and final instruction, prayer is key in confronting the spiritual warfare described in 6:12. Paul encourages the Ephesian believers to pray constantly and persistently in 6:18.

Read 1 Thessalonians 5:16–18, Philippians 4:6–7, and Colossians 4:2–4. What does it mean to pray "at all times" or "without ceasing"?

_____

_____

_____

According to Thessalonians 5:16–18, what is the focus of rejoicing and prayer? In what ways can your prayer and praise keep your focus on Christ?

_____

_____

_____

Earlier, Paul wrote that he consistently remembers the Ephesian believers in his prayers (see Eph 1:15–21). Now he asks that they pray for him (6:19–20). What did Paul pray for? What did he request prayer for? Think of ways you can incorporate prayers for others into your daily routine.

_____

_____

_____

Paul was imprisoned ("an ambassador in chains"; 6:20) when he wrote Ephesians, yet he did not ask the Ephesians to pray for his release. Instead, Paul prayed for boldness to proclaim the gospel. How does Paul's request encourage you to "be strong" and "stand firm" in your spiritual life?

_____

_____

_____

CONCLUSION

The Christian life can be confusing. We are called to be selfless, compassionate, and forgiving, yet courageous in taking a stand for our beliefs and proclaiming the gospel boldly. We must show grace to the broken people we encounter, yet distance ourselves from their sin and wrestle against the spiritual forces that influence them (Eph 5:7–14; 6:11–12). How do you balance a Christ-like love for others with a holy hatred of sin?

Only God's wisdom and understanding can empower us to live in His image (5:15, 17). Only His Spirit can strengthen us to walk as new creatures in Christ Jesus, created for good works as we are filled with the fullness of God (2:10; 3:16–19; 5:18). May God give you a spirit of wisdom and a greater revelation of Him. May this knowledge permeate your life as you display the grace of God to others while boldly proclaiming the gospel.

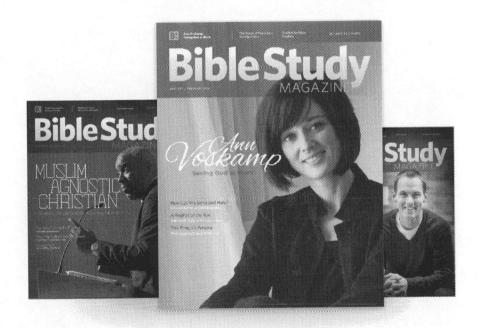